POPULAR CULTURE

A VIEW FROM THE PAPARAZZI

Orlando Bloom

John Legend

Kelly Clarkson

Lindsay Lohan

Johnny Depp

Mandy Moore

Hilary Duff

Ashlee and
Jessica Simpson

Will Ferrell

Justin
Timberlake

Jake Gyllenhaal

Paris and
Nicky Hilton

Owen and
Luke Wilson

LeBron James

Tiger Woods

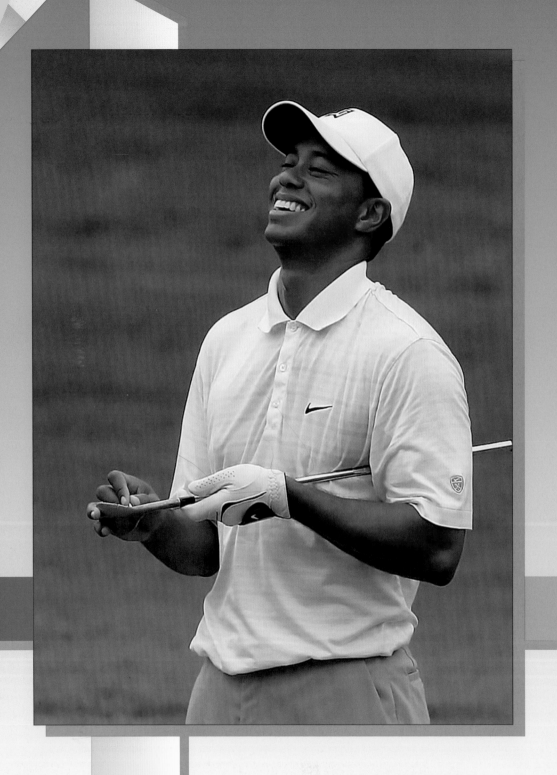

Tiger Woods

Jim Gallagher

Mason Crest Publishers

Tiger Woods

FRONTIS
Although Tiger Woods has dominated the professional golf tour for more than a decade, he constantly seeks to improve his game.

DEDICATION
To my Godchild, Delaney Turnbull, who will be a much better golfer than I.

Produced by 21st Century Publishing and Communications, Inc.

MASON CREST PUBLISHERS INC.
370 Reed Road
Broomall, Pennsylvania 19008
(866) MCP-BOOK (toll free)
www.masoncrest.com

Printed in the United States.

First Printing

9 8 7 6 5 4 3 2 1

Library of Congress Cataloging-in-Publication Data

Gallagher, Jim, 1969–
    Tiger Woods / Jim Gallagher.
        p. cm. — (Pop culture : a view from the papparazzi)
    Includes bibliographical references and index.
    Hardback edition: ISBN-13: 978-1-4222-0211-1
    Paperback edition: ISBN-13: 978-1-4222-0366-8
 1. Woods, Tiger—Juvenile literature. 2. Golfers—United States—Biography—
Juvenile literature.   I. Title.
 GV964.W66G35 2008
 796.352092—dc22
 [B]   2007020685

Publisher's notes:
- All quotations in this book come from original sources, and contain the spelling and grammatical inconsistencies of the original text.

- The Web sites mentioned in this book were active at the time of publication. The publisher is not responsible for Web sites that have changed their addresses or discontinued operation since the date of publication. The publisher will review and update the Web site addresses each time the book is reprinted.

CONTENTS

Tiger Woods has established himself as the greatest golfer of his generation. He has won more than 50 tournaments, earned over $60 million on the PGA Tour, and has set numerous records. But Tiger is not willing to rest on his past accomplishments and remains driven to stay atop the golf world.

1

The Toughest Challenge

Tiger Woods has established himself as one of the greatest golfers of all time. In his first 11 seasons as a professional, he won more than 50 tournaments. He has also set the Professional Golf Association (PGA) Tour's record for highest earnings in a career, with more than $69 million by the end of 2007.

Tiger is one of the world's highest-paid athletes. In addition to his tournament winnings, he earns tens of millions of dollars each year by appearing in advertisements for numerous products. However, money has never been Tiger's primary motivation. Since joining the PGA Tour in mid-1996, Tiger's goal has been simple: to become the greatest golfer of all time.

The Quest for Golf Immortality

The reputations of golf's greatest players are generally measured by the number of major championships, or **majors**, each has won during his career. The majors are the four most important and prestigious golf tournaments played each season. The four majors are the Masters Championship, held in April; the U.S. Open in June; the British Open in July; and the PGA Championship in August. By that standard, the greatest golfer is the legendary Jack Nicklaus, who won 18 majors during his long career. At the start of the 2006 season Walter Hagen, a great golf star of the 1920s, was second on the all-time list with 11 major victories.

In 2005 Tiger moved into third place on the list by winning his ninth and tenth majors. As the 2006 season began, he hoped to gain more ground on Nicklaus's record. But there was another reason Tiger wanted to make a good showing in the majors that year. His father, Earl Woods, was dying of **prostate cancer**, and by the spring of 2006 it was clear he would not live much longer. Earl had taught Tiger how to play golf, and had trained him to handle the pressure of competition as a teenager. The two had a very close relationship, and Tiger hoped to dedicate another major win to his dying dad.

Earl was so sick that, for the first time, he could not attend the Masters Championship at Augusta National Golf Club in Georgia to watch his son play. Instead, he watched the 2006 tournament on television. Tiger desperately wanted to win, and on the last day of the tournament he found himself close to the lead. But unlike other tournaments, Tiger was not able to mount a charge, and he finished tied for third, three strokes behind rival Phil Mickelson. Afterward, Tiger's **caddy** Steve Williams talked about several missed shots that would have made a difference in Tiger's final score. Williams said, "It was the only time I saw him try too hard."

Tiger himself later admitted to *Sports Illustrated* that he was pressing on the last day of the Masters because he was thinking about his dying father:

❝It was my last round that my Dad ever watched me play. . . . If I could have given him one last shot, some positive memories before he goes, it would have been huge.❞

Tiger appears at a 2004 press conference with his father, Earl, who taught Tiger how to play golf when he was a child. "Tiger will be a more important figure outside of golf than in it," Earl proudly declared soon after Tiger became a professional golfer. "He will make his mark on world history."

A Devastating Loss

Three weeks after Tiger's disappointing finish at the Masters, on May 3, 2006, Earl Woods died. The grief-stricken golfer posted a message about his father on his website:

> **"My dad was my best friend and greatest role model, and I will miss him deeply. I'm overwhelmed when I think of all of the great things he accomplished in his life.... I wouldn't be where I am today without him."**

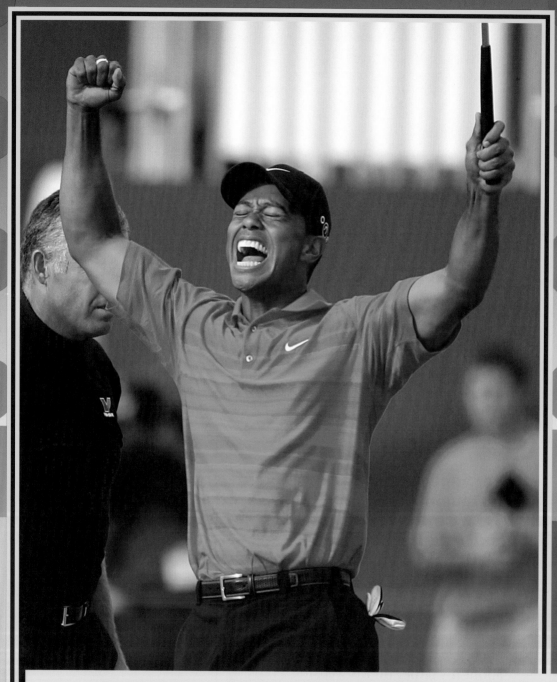

An emotional Tiger celebrates after winning the 135th British Open Championship on July 23, 2006. "I just miss my dad so much," Tiger told the BBC afterward. "I wish he could have been here to witness this. He enjoyed watching me grind out major wins and this would have brought a smile to his face."

Tiger took nine weeks off from competing on the PGA Tour to mourn for his father and spend time with his family. He returned in June for the year's second major, the U.S. Open, but it was clear that he was not ready to play. In professional golf tournaments, after the first two days only the top half of the field gets to continue. The rest are **cut**, or sent home. Tiger shot 12 over **par** for the first two rounds. It was the first time he missed the cut in a major as a professional.

An Emotional Victory

Many golf observers wondered whether Tiger would be able to get over his father's death. But three weeks later, Tiger showed that he was still the greatest golfer in the world. On the first day of the British Open, he took the lead. Over the next three days he held off all challengers. When he tapped in his final **putt** on Sunday for a two-shot victory and his 11th major win, the normally composed golfer hugged his caddy, then his wife Elin, with tears running down his face. It was an incredible, emotional, moment. Tiger later said:

> **"I'm kind of the one who bottles things up a little bit and moves on. But at that moment, it just came pouring out. And of all the things that my father has meant to me and the game of golf, I just wish he would have seen it one more time."**

Tiger would go on to win a second major, the 2006 PGA Tournament, and finished the year with six straight wins and nearly $10 million in earnings. In December Tiger was named the PGA Tour's Player of the Year for the eighth time. Although professionally 2006 was a very satisfying season, when Tiger was asked how he would remember the year, he responded by saying simply, "a loss."

Five-year-old Tiger practices with his dad. "Pop would remind me how important it is to prepare for life's challenges," Tiger later said. "But when he would tell me, 'Son, you get out of [golf] what you put into it,' I understood exactly what he meant: That no one is going to give you anything in life unless you work hard."

2

Growing up with Golf

Eldrick Thon Woods was born on December 30, 1975, to Earl and Kultida Woods of Cypress, California, a suburb of Los Angeles. His father, Earl Woods, had served in the American army during the Vietnam War. Earl nicknamed his infant son "Tiger" in honor of a Vietnamese friend that he had fought with named Vuong Dang Phong.

Tiger's **ethnic** background is mixed—his father is one-half African American, one-quarter Chinese, and one-quarter Native American, while his mother is one-half Thai, one-quarter Chinese, and one-quarter Dutch. (To describe his ethnicity, Tiger made up the term "Cablinasian"—caucasian, black, American Indian, and Asian).

Earl Woods did not start playing golf until just before he retired from the military as a lieutenant colonel. Like many people Earl considered golf a game played only by wealthy white men at country clubs. However, Earl soon became addicted to the challenge of golf, and began playing regularly on the public golf courses near his home. When he was not playing, he practiced his swing inside his garage by hitting golf balls off an artificial grass mat and into a net.

An Early Start

As a six-month-old infant, Tiger loved to sit in a high chair in the garage and watch his father practice. Soon, Tiger was hitting balls himself using a plastic putter. Earl later said,

> **It was uncanny the way he could emulate my swing. It was like looking at a mirror image of myself.**

Not long after he could stand, Tiger was hitting golf balls with a toy club on the lawn of the family's house. Earl eventually had a golf club made that Tiger could handle, and let him hit balls at the local course.

By the time Tiger was three years old, his golfing skills were attracting media attention. A local television station did a short story about him. Other stories followed after he won a golf competition against 10 and 11 year olds. He even appeared on a 1978 segment of the *Mike Douglas Show*, where he practiced his putting with famed comedian and avid golfer Bob Hope. When Tiger was five, he appeared on the nationally syndicated television show *That's Incredible*, and *Golf Digest* published a feature article about him.

Although Earl always encouraged his son's interest in golf, Tiger has said that his father never pushed him to play. Tiger always wanted to practice, and would beg his father to take him to the golf course after school. Kultida Woods often had to put her foot down, insisting that Tiger finish his schoolwork or complete his chores before he could play.

Tiger always gives his parents credit for making him the person he became. During a 1996 press conference, he said of Kultida and Earl:

> **They have raised me well and I truly believe have taught me to accept full responsibility for all aspects of my life.**

Tiger poses with his mother, Kultida, after his victory at the 2000 U.S. Open. Both Kultida and Earl Woods have always been proud of Tiger's accomplishments. "When my son wants to achieve something, nothing distracts him," Kultida told reporters. "I don't know why. It's just in him. He's a special kid, and that is the most special thing about him."

Training a Tiger

As Tiger grew older he began working with professional golf coaches, who were able to teach him more about the techniques of the game than his father could. However, Earl continued to play golf with Tiger and always tried to help him improve. Earl understood that if Tiger wanted to compete at a high level in golf, he would have to be very tough mentally.

When Tiger was about 12 years old, his father began trying to rattle his son when they were playing. Earl would cough or jingle change in his pocket just before Tiger putted, or would make noises when his son was in the middle of a swing. Concentration is very important in golf, and small distractions can throw off a player's game. Tiger soon learned how to block out everything around him and focus only on hitting his shot. He later commented about his father's unorthodox training techniques,

> **"He'd push me to the breaking point, then back off, push me, then back off. It was wild, but you got to think that it helped. I'd get angry sometimes. But I knew it was for the betterment of me. That's what learning is all about, right?"**

The hard work paid off. When Tiger was 15 he won the U.S. Junior Amateur Championship, a national golf competition for boys under the age of 18. The annual event draws several thousand of the best young golfers in the country. Tiger was the youngest winner ever. The next year, Tiger became the youngest golfer ever to play in a PGA Tour event, the 1992 Los Angeles Open. He also became the first player to repeat as Junior Amateur Champion. He would win an **unprecedented** third Junior Amateur title in 1993.

U.S. Amateur Champion

In 1994 18-year-old Tiger was too old for junior competition. Instead, he would have to test his skills at the U.S. Amateur Championship, the most prestigious tournament in the United States for male amateur golfers. Many of the country's best golfers first came to prominence with their victories in the tournament, including Arnold Palmer (in 1954), Jack Nicklaus (1959 and 1961), and Phil Mickelson (1990). Tiger joined their ranks with a victory that was notable for two reasons: he

Tiger blasts out of a sand trap during an amateur competition in 1994. He had an amazing amateur career, and remains the only golfer to win three consecutive U.S. Junior Amateur titles and three consecutive U.S. Amateur titles. Tiger also turned in strong performances as an amateur in the 1995 Masters and 1996 British Open.

was the youngest winner ever, as well as the first black golfer to win the championship. After the event, Tiger addressed those who were calling him a great African-American golfer, and clearly stated his goals for the future:

> **"I don't want to be the greatest *minority* golfer ever; I want to be the greatest golfer ever. I want to be the Michael Jordan of golf."**

Later in 1994 Tiger received valuable experience when he was invited to join an American team of amateur golfers for the World Amateur Championships. Tiger flew to France for the tournament and held his own against some of the best amateur golfers in the world. Thanks to his low scoring, the U.S. team won the event for the first time in five years.

Going to College

Although Tiger was a nationally known golfer, in many ways his life was pretty normal. In high school he enjoyed playing sports and video games with his friends. He was an excellent student, winning the Dial Award as the top scholar-athlete in the nation in 1994.

After graduating from Anaheim Western High School, he entered Stanford University, one of the country's most prestigious schools, in the fall of 1994. Tiger received a **scholarship**, which meant that Stanford would pay for his education if he played on the school's golf team. Stanford had one of the best teams in the country, which was one reason Tiger was interested in the school. The Cardinal had won the NCAA Championship in 1994, and hoped that Tiger would help them repeat as champs in his freshman year.

In his first college season, 1995, Tiger did everything he was asked to do. He won several tournaments, set a school record for lowest scoring average, and finished fifth overall at the NCAA Championships. Although Stanford placed second in the NCAA, Tiger was named First Team All-American for his great play throughout the season.

Playing With the Pros

The year 1995 brought new accomplishments as well. By winning the 1994 U.S. Amateur Championship, Tiger had qualified to play in one of the most prestigious golf tournaments, the Masters at Augusta National

Golf Club in Georgia. It was a historic moment, as Tiger was just the fourth African-American golfer to appear in the Masters (the others were Lee Elder in 1975, Calvin Peete in 1983, and Jim Thorpe in 1988). Although he did not finish among the leaders, Tiger did make the cut. He finished 41st, recording the lowest score by an amateur that year.

Later that summer, Tiger was invited to play in another major, the British Open. The 1995 event was held at the historic Old Course at St. Andrews, Scotland, one of the world's oldest golf courses. Once again, Tiger made the cut, proving that he belonged by shooting a respectable score of 295. Although he finished 13 strokes behind the winner, John Daly, he was ahead of many established pro golfers.

The lessons Tiger had learned playing at the Masters and U.S. Open would help him when he was ready to defend his title at the 1995 U.S. Amateur tournament. As the defending champion, everyone in the field was gunning for him. Tiger won his early matches easily. Although his semifinal and final round matches were closer, Tiger emerged as the champion again.

Tiger would win the U.S. Amateur title again in 1996. No other golfer had ever won the title three years in a row. He also won the NCAA men's golf championship and received the Jack Nicklaus College Player of the Year Award from the College Golf Foundation. At the British Open that July, Tiger recorded the best score by an amateur and finished tied for 22nd. After that, it seemed there was nothing left for Tiger Woods to accomplish in the world of amateur athletics.

In August 1996 Tiger announced that he would become a professional golfer. Many people praised the decision. "I have so much admiration for this kid. He is one of my idols," said basketball superstar Michael Jordan. "I am in awe of what he's done. He certainly has the tools and work ethic to truly innovate the game."

3

Turning Pro

I n the summer of 1996, practically everyone who followed golf was wondering whether Tiger Woods would become a professional. In August *Golf Digest* pictured the young athlete on the cover, under the headline "Will He or Won't He?" Respected pros like Greg Norman and Ernie Els felt Tiger was ready for the PGA Tour. Els told the media:

> **"He can't accomplish anything more in amateur golf. He's won everything. He's done everything. If he stays amateur, his level is not going to go up. [On the pro tour]**

he's learning quicker. Give him two years, and he'll be as good as anybody.**"**

Tiger made his decision after winning the U.S. Amateur title for the third time. On August 27, 1996, he held a press conference in the club-house of the Brown Deer Golf Course in Milwaukee to announce that he would become a professional golfer. The next day, Tiger signed lucrative contracts with Nike and Titleist. The companies agreed to pay him $60 million over five years to **endorse** their products.

A Tough Road

Although the deals ensured his financial security, there was no guarantee that Tiger would be allowed to stay on the PGA Tour. To earn a spot on the Tour, golfers must pass a rigorous qualifying school. Of the thousands of players who enter, only the top 30 win their Tour card, which entitles them to play in PGA events for a year. Once on the tour, players must finish among the top 125 money-winners in order to receive their Tour card for the following year. Otherwise, the player must go through the qualifying school again.

Because of the hype surrounding Tiger, tournament sponsors were interested in having him play at their events. He was offered **sponsors' exemptions**, which would allow him to compete in PGA Tour events during 1996 even though he did not have his Tour card. However, the 1996 season was nearly over. In order to avoid having to go through the difficult qualifying school, Tiger would have to win about $150,000 in the eight events left on the schedule. This would rank him among the top 125 money-winners for the year.

This goal seemed impossible, especially after Tiger finished his first tournament, the Greater Milwaukee Open, tied for 60th place. The $2,544 he earned there ranked him 344th on the money list. Tiger soon found his groove, though. He placed 11th at the Canadian Open the next week, and the $37,500 paycheck moved him up to 204th on the money list.

At both tournaments, huge audiences showed up to watch Tiger play. Many minorities and young people wanted to see Tiger, and extra tickets had to be printed to handle the overflow crowds. A series of television advertisements that the young golfer did for Nike increased his visibility and fueled the hype surrounding his first pro appearances, sometimes referred to as "Tiger-mania."

A huge crowd watches Tiger hit a shot. From the time he announced his decision to turn pro, he revitalized the sport of golf. There was an enormous demand for tickets to tournaments in which Tiger had agreed to play, and the large galleries that followed him around often included many people who had not previously watched golf.

Ready to Win

In Tiger's next tournament, the Quad Cities, he held the lead entering the final day of play. However, he played two holes badly on Sunday and wound up in a tie for fifth place, earning a $42,150 check that moved him up to 166th on the money list. Afterward, Tiger's coach Butch Harmon commented:

> **The one thing he's going to learn from this is how hard it is to win a tour event. The way things were going, I don't think he thought it was too hard. Even though I wish he had won the tournament, in the long run this may be better for him. He'll come away from this realizing that it's not easy to win out here, no matter who you are.**

The next week, Tiger finished third at the B.C. Open. The check for $58,000 moved him up to 128th on the money list. After taking a week off, Tiger ensured that he would play on the PGA Tour in 1997 when he won the Las Vegas Invitational, beating Tour veteran Davis Love III in a playoff. The winner's share of $297,000 increased his earnings for the year to $437,194 and moved him all the way up to 40th place on the money list.

In the last two events of the season, Tiger finished third at the Texas Open and won the Disney Classic. That moved him up to 23rd place on the money list, and qualified Tiger for a spot in the season-ending Tour Championship, a tournament open to the top 30 players. Tiger finished tied for 24th and won another $55,800, bringing his total for the year to $790,594. It had been an incredible season, and was topped off by Tiger's selection as the PGA Tour's Rookie of the Year.

All Eyes on Tiger

With his first professional season under his belt, Tiger was ready to begin working toward a place in the record books as the 1997 season began. He picked up where he had left off in the season-opening tournament, the Mercedes Championship, in January 1997. Tiger finished tied with the 1996 PGA Player of the Year, Tom Lehman, then beat Lehman in a playoff.

After playing several other tournaments, in February Tiger traveled to Thailand to appear in the Asian Honda Classic. Although the Classic is not an official PGA Tour event, Tiger wanted to play because of his mother, who is from Thailand. He was greeted like a rock star, as police had to hold back the huge crowd that gathered to see him at the airport. Tiger showed what all the fuss was about by winning the Asian Honda Classic by 20 strokes. Tiger then played a tournament in Australia before returning to the United States.

Asian fans seek Tiger's autograph after he completes the first day of the Asian Honda Classic in 1997. Tiger agreed to play in the tournament because it was held in Thailand, his mother's home country. He was greeted like a rock star, with fans and local journalists following him everywhere he went.

Tiger fires a shot toward the green during the 1997 Masters. The 21-year-old's performance in the Masters exceeded even the high expectations of golf fans. After a slow start he gained the lead, and by the final day of the tournament the only question that remained was the size of Tiger's margin of victory.

Other players on the PGA Tour were starting to admit that Tiger's laser-like focus on winning made him the player to beat in most tournaments. At the Bay Hill Invitational in March, two-time Tour winner Billy Andrade said, "This kid is 21 years old, and he's the best player in the world. He's not happy finishing eighth or sixth or second. He wants to win." Tom Lehman commented:

> **❝I kind of get the impression that we're all chasing Tiger. I think that he's good for the game. I think that people are aware of the fact that there is a new kid on the block who is extremely talented.❞**

A Historic Masters Victory

On Thursday, April 10, 1997, Tiger Woods teed off at Augusta National Golf Course for the first round of the Masters. His first drive was off-course, landing in the high grass along the fairway. Tiger made a bogey on the first hole, and was four strokes over par after his first nine holes. After that Tiger turned his game around. He played the back nine holes in six shots below par, nearly breaking the course record. He finished with a 70, good for fourth place and just three strokes behind the leader. He continued his hot play on Friday, shooting a 66 that gave him a three-stroke lead.

On Saturday Tiger pulled away from the field. By the time he **birdied** the 11th hole it was clear that he was going to win the Masters. He finished the day 15 strokes under par, and held a nine-shot lead. The only question in most people's minds was whether he could break the record for lowest score in the tournament. Golf legend Jack Nicklaus had set the mark of 271, 17 strokes under par, in 1965, and Ray Floyd had matched it in 1976.

Earl and Kultida Woods were on hand Sunday as Tiger teed off. He was wearing a red shirt, as he always does in the final round of tournaments. (Tiger has said the color represents aggressiveness.) Tiger's only challenge was the record, and as he walked up the 18th fairway, surrounded by an enormous crowd of cheering people, he knew it was in reach. When Tiger sank a putt to par the hole, the audience cheered wildly. Tiger had dominated an elite field of golfers in the Masters, winning by 12 strokes. No golfer had won a major tournament by that large a margin in more than 130 years. In addition to finishing with a 270 to break the scoring record, Tiger set several other records, including becoming the youngest Masters winner ever at just 21 years old.

But for most people, Tiger's accomplishment was notable because he was the first African American to win a major championship. That the victory came on a historic golf course in Georgia where blacks had not been permitted to play until the mid-1970s, and where blacks had not been admitted as members until 1990, made Tiger's win all the more significant. Lee Elder, the first African American to play in

Nick Faldo, winner of the 1996 Masters, places the fabled green jacket on Tiger's shoulders, April 13, 1997. Golf legend Jack Nicklaus called Tiger's record-setting performance "incredible," while Tom Watson, another of golf's great players, commented that Tiger was like "a boy among men—and the boy showed the men how to play."

the Masters, spoke to reporters about the importance of Tiger's 1997 Masters victory:

> **❝This is so significant [to our society]. . . . It's such a great day for golf. It's such a great day for all people. . . . After today, we will have a situation where no one will even turn their head to notice when a black person walks to the first tee.❞**

Tiger became emotional as he hugged his father after sinking the final putt. A short time later, he grinned as the famous green jacket given to Masters champions was slipped onto his shoulders. "I've always dreamed of coming up 18 and winning," he said. "But I've never thought this far through the ceremony."

A Great First Season

The Masters win was the highlight of Tiger's year. But there was still plenty of golf to be played, and Tiger found himself close to the lead in nearly every tournament. By the end of the year he had won four PGA events and earned more than $2 million. This figure not only led the money list, it set a new record for most money won in a season. His consistent play enabled Tiger to rise to the top spot in the world golf rankings. For his accomplishments, he was named the 1997 PGA Player of the Year.

Tiger lines up a putt. Between 1999 and 2002 Tiger would dominate the PGA Tour, leading the tour in winnings each year and racking up a total of 27 victories. Even his fellow professionals were in awe of his ability. "The only thing that can stop Tiger from winning is Tiger," commented one competitor, Jesper Parnevik.

4

Years of Dominance

In 1998 Tiger only won one PGA tournament, although he did finish fourth on the money list with more than $1.8 million in earnings. For any other player, this would have been a great season. But the expectations were so high for Tiger that many people started talking about his "slump."

One reason Tiger did not win as many tournaments in 1998 was that he was trying to improve his golf swing. The level of competition on the PGA Tour is so high that one or two bad shots can be the difference between winning and losing. Although Tiger knew that when he was playing well no one could beat him, he also realized that in order to win regularly he needed a more consistent swing that would enable him to avoid those bad shots.

Butch Harmon, Tiger's coach, is one of the most respected golf teachers in the world, and he started working on the young golfer's new swing a few months after the 1997 Masters. Harmon said:

"We began by talking about it, asking ourselves, 'what do we need to do to change this?' . . . It was obvious he was having trouble controlling his distance, controlling his trajectory under pressure. . . . I started to formulate a plan [but] it had to be Tiger's decision to change, obviously."

Relearning how to swing a golf club was not the only big change in Tiger's life. During 1998 he began dating Joanna Jagoda, an attractive blond student at the University of California-Santa Barbara. The two were introduced at that year's Nissan Open, and by the fall she was appearing with Tiger at public functions. She even traveled with him to Australia for an international tournament. However, Tiger preferred to keep his personal life private, and rarely spoke about their relationship with reporters. "She hasn't gone through this [media attention] enough yet," he said.

A Breakout Year

It is very difficult for a player to make major changes to the way he swings his clubs and still remain competitive at a high level. Throughout 1998 Tiger struggled to learn what Harmon wanted him to do, but by June 1999, when he won Jack Nicklaus's Memorial Tournament by two strokes over Vijay Singh, it was clear that Tiger had mastered the new swing. He was about to enter a period in which he would dominate his sport like no golfer had ever done before.

Nicklaus, arguably the greatest professional golfer of all time, could see the changes in Tiger's game, and he predicted that the young man would be very tough to beat. He told the media:

"[Tiger] has the ability to do things that nobody else can do. And yet he's got a short game that where if he makes mistakes, he can correct it. That's what's so phenomenal."

Nicklaus's prediction came true, as Tiger finished 1999 with eight victories on the PGA Tour. No one had won that many events in a

In order to win regularly on the PGA Tour, Tiger knew that his golf swing would have to become more consistent. During 1998 and 1999 he spent thousands of hours practicing the new swing that he and coach Butch Harmon had developed. All of the hard work would lead to the most productive period of Tiger's career.

season in 25 years. The most satisfying of these wins came at the PGA Championship in mid-August, when Tiger held off Spaniard Sergio Garcia by a stroke for his second major victory. Tiger also won a record $6.6 million, completely destroying the old mark. He also won three non-PGA events and led the Tour in scoring with an average of 68.43 strokes per round.

Tiger watches a tee shot during a 1999 tournament. That year he won eight PGA events, a feat that no one had accomplished since Johnny Miller in 1974, and regained his ranking as the number one golfer in the world. Thanks to these exploits Tiger was named PGA Tour Player of the Year for the second time.

In September 1999 Tiger played for the Ryder Cup, a tournament held every two years. He competed on the American team against a team of British and European golfers. Tiger did not play well on the first two days of the tournament, and the Americans were losing 10 to 6 as they entered the final day. However, he won his match on Sunday, helping the American team make a remarkable comeback to win the Ryder Cup.

Dominating His Opponents

Greater things were yet to come in 2000. Tiger beat one of the Tour's best golfers, Ernie Els, in a playoff in the year's first event, the Mercedes Championship, then won his second tournament of 2000, the AT&T Pebble Beach National Pro-Am. He now had won six straight times dating back to 1999. Phil Mickelson finally ended Tiger's streak at the Buick Invitational, but Tiger remained red hot. He came right back to win his next event, the Bay Hill Invitational.

Tiger shakes hands with Ernie Els at a tournament. Since the mid-1990s Els has regularly been among the top five players in the world, and has won three major tournaments. Yet despite tough competition from Els and other great golfers like Phil Mickelson and Vijay Singh, Tiger has remained golf's most dominant player.

For most players, finishing in the top five in a major would be a great accomplishment. For Tiger, his fifth-place finish in the 2000 Masters was a big disappointment. Tiger had struggled in the first two rounds of the Masters, although he turned things around on the weekend and pulled himself into contention.

That early struggle would not happen in the next major, the U.S. Open. Tiger shot a 65 in the first round and never looked back, winning the event by 15 strokes and setting a new record for lowest score in the tournament. A few weeks later, at the historic St. Andrews course in Scotland, Tiger won the British Open by eight strokes. He had now won each of the four majors, an accomplishment known as the **career grand slam**. Only Gene Sarazen, Ben Hogan, Nicklaus, and Gary Player had previously achieved the career grand slam.

Ernie Els, who finished second to Tiger in the 2000 U.S. Open and British Open, commented on the young golfer's dominance. He told reporters:

"The guy's 24 years old and he's lapping us in the majors every time, it looks like. I'm supposed to be getting to my prime. I'm 30 years old but I'm going against a guy who's fearless and with so much confidence that it's going to be tough to beat him. We just have to hope he's off. At the moment, he's streets ahead of us."

The Greatest Year Ever

Tiger was not through. At the 2000 PGA Championship, he again broke the scoring record, shooting 18 under par. However, a relatively unknown golfer named Bob May matched Tiger stroke for stroke, tying for the lead and forcing a dramatic playoff. On their third playoff hole Tiger hit a perfect shot with his pitching wedge that landed less than two feet away from the cup. When he sank the putt Tiger had won his third major of the year—something only one other golfer, Ben Hogan back in 1953, had ever done.

Many people agreed that Tiger's 2000 season was among the best of all time. He won nine tournaments and set 27 PGA Tour records. One of these was a new earnings mark, as he won $9.1 million, shattering his own record set the previous year. In less than five full seasons on the

Tiger holds the Claret Jug after winning the 2000 British Open on the historic course at St. Andrews, Scotland, which is regarded as the worldwide "home of golf." The victory was Tiger's fourth career major, as well as his second major of the year; he would add another to his total by winning the 2000 PGA Championship.

PGA Tour, Tiger had already won more money in his career than any other professional golfer in history.

Off the course Tiger was doing very well financially. In the summer of 2000 he renegotiated his contract with Nike, signing a new five-year deal worth $100 million. Tiger also made lucrative deals to endorse Buick cars from General Motors, American Express credit cards, and many other products. Thanks to all of his endorsement deals, Tiger was the highest-paid athlete in the world.

The Tiger Slam

But making a lot of money was never Tiger's main goal. Winning tournaments, particularly major championships, is where the young golfer focuses his attention. Tiger came out strong in 2001, winning two tournaments in March. The second of these victories was at the prestigious Players Championship, an event sometimes called the "fifth major."

Tiger continued his strong play into April. At the 2001 Masters he shot a 68 to take the lead in the third round. On Sunday he was paired with Phil Mickelson, who was ranked second in the world. But Mickelson faded in the final round, and Tiger won his second Masters by two strokes.

For the first time in golf history, a single player possessed the trophies for all four majors at the same time. Golf writers nicknamed this feat the "Tiger Slam." After the Masters tournament Tiger reflected on his accomplishment:

> **"When I won in '97, I hadn't been a pro a full year yet. I was a little young, a little naïve. . . . I've witnessed a lot of things since then. I have a better appreciation for winning a major championship, and to win four of them in succession, it's just so hard for me to believe, really, because there's so many things that go into it."**

The rest of 2001 was something of a disappointment. Tiger was unable to defend his titles in the other majors, finishing 12th at the U.S. Open, 25th at the British Open, and 29th at the PGA Championship. He did finish with five victories and more than $6.6 million in earnings, however, and was named PGA Player of the Year for the fourth time.

Tiger watches as executives from the credit card company American Express take part in a putting contest. After he turned pro Tiger signed lucrative contracts with American Express and other companies, including Nike, golf equipment manufacturer Titleist, General Motors, and General Mills. The income from these endorsement deals made Tiger the highest-paid athlete in the world.

Grand Slam Edition

TIGER WOODS

2001: THE YEAR OF THE TIGER

- The Major Victories
- The Early Days

What's Next?

The "grand slam edition" of a 2001 magazine about Tiger. When the young golfer won the 2001 Masters, he became the only player in golf history to hold all four major titles at the same time. Because Tiger did not win all of the tournaments in the same year, golf writers dubbed this accomplishment the "Tiger Slam."

The year was not without a shakeup in Tiger's personal life. In mid-2001 he and Joanna Jagoda broke up after two years together. Although neither was willing to discuss their breakup with the media, it seems likely that their ambitions and schedules played a large part. Tiger was constantly traveling to golf tournaments, while Jagoda was busy with her studies at Pepperdine University's law school, where she had enrolled in the fall of 2000.

Continuing to Dominate

The year 2002 brought more of the same for Tiger. In April he became just the third player to win the Masters in back-to-back seasons, and in June he won the U.S. Open by three strokes over Phil Mickelson for his eighth career major victory. Although Tiger was not a factor at the British Open—he had a terrible third round and finished 28th— he finished second in the PGA Championship. For the year, Tiger won five tournaments and nearly $7 million, and won the money title, Vardon Trophy, and Player of the Year award for the fourth year in a row.

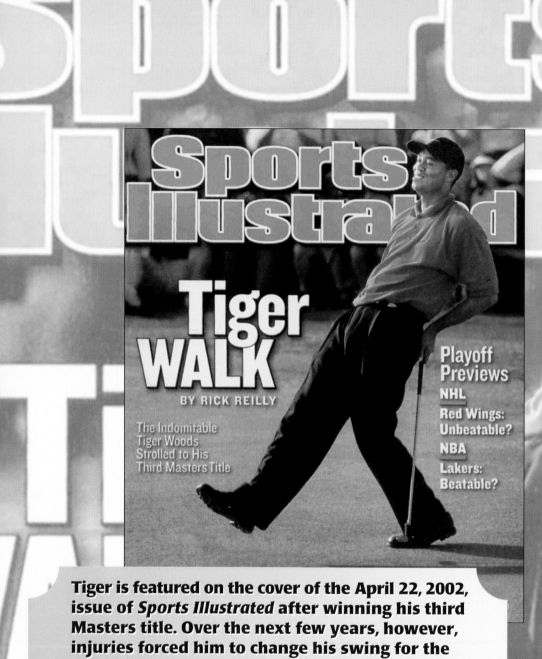

Sports Illustrated

Tiger WALK

BY RICK REILLY

The Indomitable Tiger Woods Strolled to His Third Masters Title

Playoff Previews

NHL
Red Wings: Unbeatable?

NBA
Lakers: Beatable?

Tiger is featured on the cover of the April 22, 2002, issue of *Sports Illustrated* after winning his third Masters title. Over the next few years, however, injuries forced him to change his swing for the second time as a professional. This led to a period in which Tiger could no longer dominate golf the way he once had.

5

Closer Competition

By the end of 2002 Tiger Woods was far and away the best player in golf. But his period of dominance was about to come to an end. Over the next few years, the victories would not come as easily, and for a short time other golfers would surpass Tiger as the game's best player.

Although the new swing Tiger developed with Butch Harmon had made him incredibly successful, it also placed great stresses on his body. Tiger had problems with his left knee throughout 2002, and at the end of the season he had surgery to repair torn tendons. The surgery caused him to miss the first tournament of the 2003 season.

Although Tiger did win five tournaments in 2003, including the Accenture Match Play championship, a head-to-head competition against some of the best players in golf, he was disappointed with the season. His best finish in the majors was a tie for fourth at the British Open, and surprisingly he was not in contention in the other three events. He won over $6.6 million, but fell to second on the money list behind Vijay Singh. Despite this, Tiger was again named the PGA's Player of the Year.

Tiger's personal life took a significant turn in 2003 with his engagement to Elin Nordegren, a Swedish model he had met two years earlier. Tiger has always preferred to keep his personal life private, so few people knew about the relationship before the engagement was announced.

Under Construction

Tiger understood that in order to remain at the top of the golf world, he would need to remake his swing again so that it would place less stress on his body. By the time the 2004 season began, he had fired Butch Harmon. In March 2004 he started working with a new teacher named Hank Haney, who had very different ideas about Tiger's swing.

Tiger knew that as he learned how to swing his clubs the way Haney taught, his game would suffer at first. After all, that had happened in 1998. Tiger won just one tournament in 2004, and he dropped to fourth on the money list. His best finish in a major was ninth at the British Open. In September 2004, after holding the top spot in the world golf rankings for a record 264 consecutive weeks, Tiger lost the position to Vijay Singh.

To most observers Tiger seemed to be stuck in a serious slump. Many golf analysts felt that other talented golfers like Singh, Phil Mickelson, and Ernie Els had finally caught up to Tiger. Even Nicklaus felt that other pros had improved compared to Tiger, saying at the 2004 Masters:

"All of a sudden, you can probably name a half a dozen players that have come out here in the last couple of years that have given Tiger a pretty good run, and are going to continue to. Plus some of the older guys, who have finally learned how to win more. I think definitely the major tournaments are more open today."

Sailors watch Tiger hit golf balls inside an aircraft carrier's hanger bay during a 2004 exhibition. The 2004 season was one of Tiger's worst, as he won only one tournament and lost his number-one ranking. Yet he remained confident, telling reporters after finishing tied for 22nd at the 2004 Masters, "I'm so close to putting it all together."

For Tiger, a highlight of 2004 was his marriage to Elin Nordegren on October 5 on a beach in Barbados. Among the guests were former NBA stars Michael Jordan and Charles Barkley, talk show host Oprah Winfrey, and tennis stars Venus and Serena Williams. After the lavish ceremony, Tiger and Elin spent their honeymoon cruising the Caribbean on Tiger's 155-foot luxury yacht, *Privacy*.

Return to Form

The 2005 season marked a return to form for Tiger, as he finally settled into a grove with his new swing. His March victory over Mickelson at the Ford Championship enabled him to regain his ranking as the world's top golfer. Although Tiger and Vijay competed for the number one spot for most of the year, by the fall of 2005 Tiger had gained a significant advantage over his rival. Tiger also regained his place atop the money list with over $10.6 million in earnings for the year.

Most importantly to Tiger, he was once again competitive at the majors. He won the 2005 Masters and British Open, finished second at the U.S. Open, and was fourth at the PGA Championship. After winning the British Open, Tiger said:

> **"I've been criticized for the last couple of years. 'Why would I change my game?' This is why. . . . The drive is always to get better. You can always get better, no matter what."**

Taking a Break

At the end of the 2005 season, Tiger decided to take a six-week break. For one 24-day stretch he did not even pick up a golf club, which is very unusual for Tiger. One reason for the long vacation from the game was that he wanted to spend some time with his father. Earl Woods had been in poor health for several years. He had developed prostate cancer in 1998, and although radiation treatment pushed the cancer into remission, it eventually returned. By 2004 the cancer had spread throughout his body, and by the end of 2005 Earl's condition was grave. Tiger explained:

> **"He's my dad, and I love him to death. He's my best friend, and anytime [I] can spend that much time [with him], especially when he wasn't feeling all that well, it meant the world to me."**

Tiger walks toward the green on the last day of the 2005 Buick Invitational, an event that he won with a 16-under-par score to kick off the season. Afterward, he credited the new swing for the victory, telling *Sports Illustrated*, "My mechanics are sound enough now that . . . I could make birdies."

At the end of 2005, Tiger purchased a $40 million estate on Jupiter Island in Florida. The 10-acre property included an enormous mansion and a dock for his yacht.

Saying Goodbye

The long layoff from golf did not seem to affect Tiger's game. He won his first two tournaments of 2006, and seemed to be ready for the

Masters. However, although Tiger got close to the lead on Sunday he was not able to mount his typical charge, and he finished tied for third.

Three weeks later Earl Woods died. At the U.S. Open a few weeks later, a grieving Tiger told reporters:

> **"I'm here to compete and play and try to win this championship. I know that Dad would still want me to grind it and give it my best, and that's what I always do. That's what I will certainly try to do this week."**

It was clear from the start that Tiger's heart was not in the game, though. On each of the first two holes he missed short putts for par. He

After his father's death, Tiger was unable to focus on golf for several weeks, and the rust showed in his first tournament after the layoff. Tiger's victory at the 2006 British Open proved that he was still the man to beat, however. He won over $9.9 million in 2006 and was named Player of the Year for the eighth time.

ended up shooting identical scores of 76 in the first two rounds of the tournament, and missed the cut by three strokes. It was the first time he did not play during the weekend of a major since he had turned pro in 1996.

Getting Back Into the Game

Tiger took two more weeks off before appearing in another tournament, the Western Open. This time, it was clear to all observers that his competitive fire was back. He shot a third-round 66 to get into contention, then charged for the lead in Sunday's round, finishing a close second.

At the British Open a few weeks later, Tiger won a bittersweet victory, finishing 18 strokes under par for a two-shot victory over Chris DeMarco. Tiger became the first player to win back-to-back British Opens since Tom Watson in 1982–83. After sinking his final putt, he plucked the ball from the cup, then turned to hug his wife Elin as tears streamed down his face. Afterward, Tiger explained:

> **At that moment, it just came pouring out. I was pretty bummed out after not winning the Masters, because I knew that was the last major [my dad] was ever going to see. That one hurt a little bit. And to get this one . . . it's just unfortunate he wasn't here to see it.**

In the second half of 2006 Tiger was once again unstoppable. He won the PGA Championship for the third time, and finished the season with six straight victories. For the eighth time in his career, he was named the PGA Tour's Player of the Year.

"I don't know what the future holds for me," Tiger told reporters in March 2007. "Right now I've got a lot of golf. I've got a child on the way this July." By that time Tiger was two-thirds of the way to matching the golf record he most wants to break—Jack Nicklaus's career total of 18 major victories.

6

What the Future Holds

By any standard, Tiger Woods must be considered among the greatest golfers of all time. In 2006 he became the youngest golfer to reach 50 career victories, and he is the only player in PGA history to win at least eight times in three different seasons. He is one of only five players to have won the career grand slam.

Despite his many successes, Tiger shows no signs of slowing down. By 2007 he had won 12 major titles, a number second only to Jack Nicklaus's record 18 majors. This is a mark that Tiger greatly wishes to pass. Another record that he would one day like to beat is Sam Snead's

82 career PGA Tour victories. Tiger won his 57th PGA event in May 2007; at that point the only players between him and Sneed on the all-time list were Arnold Palmer (with 62 wins), Ben Hogan (64), and Nicklaus (73). Tiger has also said he would like to tie or break Snead's record of 11 victories in a single season.

Although Tiger wins more than any other golfer on the tour, he also plays fewer events each year than most. He says that he needs time off to help him keep his focus. He also prefers to spend extra time preparing for the majors, rather than grinding out victories on the Tour. When he is not playing in a tournament, Tiger spends hours practicing at the **driving range**. He is also an exercise nut, and maintains an intense workout schedule.

When he is not playing golf or practicing, Tiger enjoys many hobbies, including skiing, scuba diving, cooking, and fishing. He also likes playing video games and relaxing with his family and friends. He and Elin often travel on their luxury yacht *Privacy* to get away from the constant media pressure and fan attention.

Charitable Work

Since becoming a professional golfer, Tiger has been very involved in charity work. In 1996 he and his father Earl established the Tiger Woods Foundation, which operates projects for young people. Through the foundation, Tiger has conducted golf clinics for young people in many cities, especially in poorer neighborhoods where the children might not otherwise have an opportunity to play. The Tiger Woods Foundation also provides scholarships and grants to talented young people from disadvantaged communities, as well as to high school graduates who demonstrate academic excellence. Since 1996 the Foundation has given out more than $30 million in grants and scholarships.

In February 2006 Tiger was joined by former president Bill Clinton for the opening of the Tiger Woods Learning Center, a 35,000 square foot educational facility in Anaheim, California. The center will provide a unique after-school experience for thousands of students in fourth through 12th grades, providing supplemental instruction in math, science, reading, and technology. It will also give students a chance to learn more about careers in such areas as forensic science, engineering, aerospace, video production, and home design. Tiger has commented:

"With this building and hopefully subsequent buildings down the road, I think we can really make a tremendous impact on kids' lives and futures."

In order to fund these programs, Tiger runs a charity golf tournament that draws the best golfers on the PGA Tour, as well as an annual benefit concert called Tiger Jam that has featured such performers as Sting, Christina Aguilera, and Bon Jovi. In 2007 it was announced that a new PGA event, the AT&T National would be held in July near Washington, D.C., to benefit the Tiger Woods Foundation.

Through his charitable Tiger Woods Foundation, Tiger has attempted to make a difference in the lives of young people. Here, Tiger watches a young player swing during a junior golf clinic at Fort Bragg, North Carolina. The Foundation also recently opened a modern learning center intended to help young people pursue their career goals.

A New Venture

In November 2006 Tiger Woods announced that he would start a business designing golf courses, following in the footsteps of Arnold Palmer and Jack Nicklaus. The next month Tiger announced that he had been hired to build a course in the United Arab Emirates near Dubai. The course, called Al Ruwaya (an Arabic word meaning "serenity"), will be part of a larger development featuring 320 homes, a luxury hotel, and a golf academy. The course is scheduled to be finished in 2009.

Tiger and Elin Woods arrive at a reception during the 2006 Ryder Cup competition in Ireland. "Without a doubt, it helps having a partner there," Tiger says of his wife, whom he married in October 2004. "We're like a team. So it's become a lot easier. We go to tournaments together, we're in this together, it makes you stronger."

Unlike Palmer, who created a partnership with an established golf architect when he was starting out, Tiger has indicated that he will be closely involved in every stage of the construction of the Dubai course. He told *Sports Illustrated*, "I will not be hiring some guy to design a golf course. I'll be hands on and involved in it."

A Major Life Change

On June 18, 2007, Tiger's life changed significantly when Elin gave birth to their daughter, Sam Alexis Woods. In a statement on his Web site posted the next day, Tiger wrote:

> **"Both Elin and Sam are doing well and resting peacefully. . . . This is truly a special time in our lives and we look forward to introducing Sam to our family and friends over the next few weeks."**

For years Tiger has spoken about his desire to be a father, citing the influence that his own father Earl had when he was growing up. Many golf commentators have speculated on how becoming a father may change Tiger's focus on golf. Tiger has admitted that golf will take a backseat to his family life. Before the 2007 Masters, he commented:

> **"Our whole priority is to raise our child—so that will be our number one priority. . . . It's our responsibility to raise [the child] as best we possibly can, and that's going to require a lot of energy. I don't know how my preparation is going to change or not, and my playing schedule is going to change or not. These are all things that are up in the air because I really don't know."**

Whatever the future holds for Tiger Woods, it is clear that he has already left an indelible mark on the game. It seems very likely that he will continue to build on his success for many years to come.

CHRONOLOGY

1975 Eldrick Thon (Tiger) Woods is born on December 30 to Earl and Kultida Woods of Cypress, California.

1978 Tiger is invited to appear on the *Mike Douglas Show* with comedian Bob Hope.

1981 Records first hole-in-one at age six.

1983 Wins Optimist International Junior World Championship, a feat he would repeat in 1984

1991 Fifteen-year-old Tiger becomes the youngest player and first African American to win the USGA's Junior Amateur Championship.

1992 Tiger repeats at Junior Amateur champion; becomes the youngest player ever to tee off in a PGA Tournament when he appears at the Los Angeles Open.

1993 Wins his third Junior Amateur championship.

1994 Tiger becomes the youngest player ever to win the U.S. Amateur Championship.

1995 Named PAC-10 Player of the Year and an NCAA All-American while helping Stanford's golf team finish second in the NCAA; becomes the fourth African American to play in the Masters; makes the cut at the British Open; repeats as U.S. Amateur champion.

1996 Wins his third U.S. Amateur Championship; in August, announces that he will become a professional and signs endorsement deals with Nike and Titleist; wins two of his first seven events to secure a spot in the season-ending Tour Championship; named Athlete of the Year by *Sports Illustrated*.

1997 Tiger becomes the first African American and the youngest player ever to win the Masters, setting a record for lowest score in the tournament.

1998 While rebuilding his swing, Tiger has an "off year," only winning one tournament.

1999 Wins eight tournaments, including the PGA Championship, and more than $6.6 million.

2000 Tiger continues to dominate professional golf, winning nine PGA events, including the last three majors of the year.

2001 Completes the "Tiger Slam" with a victory in the Masters, becoming the first player in history to hold the trophies for all four of the majors at the same time.

2002 Tiger wins the first two majors of the year, but his grand slam bid falls short when a bad round at the British Open results in a 28th-place finish; finishes atop the PGA's money list for the fourth consecutive year.

2003 Undergoes knee surgery, then works to create a new swing that will not place as much stress on his body; although Tiger wins five times, he is shut out of the majors and finishes second on the money list.

2004 Golf writers begin to talk of a "slump" after Tiger only wins one tournament and loses the top position in the world golf rankings to Vijay Singh.

2005 Tiger regains his dominant form, winning the Masters and British Open while finishing second at the U.S. Open and tied for fourth at the PGA; recovers the top position in the world golf rankings.

2006 Earl Woods dies on May 3; Tiger wins the British Open and the PGA Championship and finishes the season with six straight victories.

2007 Tiger finishes tied for second at the Masters in April and at the U.S. Open in June.

Daughter Sam Alexis Woods is born on June 18.

ACCOMPLISHMENTS & AWARDS

Selected Awards

American Junior Golf Association Player of the Year, 1991, 1992

Pac-10 Player of the Year, 1995

NCAA First Team All-American, 1995

Stanford University Collegiate Player of the Year, 1996

PGA Tour Rookie of the Year, 1996

PGA Tour Player of the Year, 1997, 1999, 2000, 2001, 2002, 2003, 2005, 2006

ESPY Award for Best Male Athlete, 1998, 2001, 2002

PGA Tour Money Winner, 1997, 1999, 2000, 2001, 2002, 2005, 2006

Vardon Trophy, 1999, 2000, 2001, 2002, 2003, 2005

Byron Nelson Award, 1999, 2000, 2001, 2002, 2003, 2005, 2006

Mark H. McCormack Award, 1998, 1999, 2000, 2001, 2002, 2003, 2004, 2005, 2006

Associated Press Male Athlete of the Year, 1997, 1999, 2000, 2006

Laureus World Sports Awards, 2000, 2001

ESPY Award for Best Male Athlete, 2000, 2002

Golf Writers Association of America Player of the Year, 2000

Career Statistics

Year	Wins	Majors	Earnings	(Rank)
1996	2	0	$790,594	(24th)
1997	4	1	$2,066,833	(1st)
1998	1	0	$1,841,117	(4th)
1999	8	1	$6,616,585	(1st)
2000	9	3	$9,188,321	(1st)
2001	5	1	$6,687,777	(1st)
2002	5	2	$6,912,625	(1st)
2003	5	0	$6,673,413	(2nd)
2004	1	0	$5,365,472	(4th)
2005	6	2	$10,628,024	(1st)
2006	8	2	$9,941,563	(1st)
2007*	3	0	$4,885,427	
Total	57	12	$70,597,751	

*Through June 17, 2007

FURTHER READING & INTERNET RESOURCES

Books

Callahan, Tom. *In Search of Tiger: A Journey Through Golf with Tiger Woods.* New York: Crown, 2003.

Durbin, William C. *Tiger Woods.* Philadelphia: Chelsea House, 1998.

Rosaforte, Tim. *Raising the Bar: The Championship Years of Tiger Woods.* New York: St. Martin's, 2002.

Sounes, Howard. *The Wicked Game: Arnold Palmer, Jack Nicklaus, Tiger Woods, and the Business of Modern Golf.* New York: William Morrow, 2004.

Woods, Earl, and Pete McDaniel. *Training a Tiger: A Father's Guide to Raising a Winner in Both Golf and Life.* New York: HarperCollins, 1997.

Woods, Tiger. *How I Play Golf.* New York: Warner Books, 2001.

Web Sites

www.pgatour.com/
The official Web site of the PGA Tour offers a variety of golf-related stories and news items, as well as tournament statistics and links to biographies of Tiger Woods and other professional golfers.

www.tigerwoods.com
The official Web site for Tiger Woods provides a short biography, his career statistics and highlights, and links to news as well as Tiger's personal blog and a selection of golf tips.

www.twfound.org/
Information about the mission and programs of the Tiger Woods Foundation, including the organization's new Tiger Woods Learning Center, can be found at the foundation's official Web site.

www.twlc.org/
The Web site for the new Tiger Woods Learning Center includes information about the center, as well as a fun game that teaches physics through golf club design.

www.usga.org/
The United States Golf Association (USGA) has served as the national governing body of golf for the United States and its territories, as well as Mexico, since 1894. Its Web site includes information about golf rules, the history of the game, and how to play.

birdie—nickname given to a score on a particular hole that is one stroke below par for that hole.

caddy—a person who carries a golfer's clubs, and often provides advice on how to play difficult shots, during a round of golf.

career grand slam—nickname given to the feat of winning each of golf's four majors at least once during a player's career. Only a handful of golfers have achieved the career grand slam.

cut—to be eliminated from a tournament. In the typical professional golf tournament, which lasts four days, the bottom half of the field is not permitted to play on Saturday and Sunday.

driving range—an open area where golfers can practice making specific shots using different clubs, without having to walk the golf course.

endorse—to give public support to a product, often in an advertisement or by openly using or speaking about the product.

ethnic—relating to a group that shares particular physical or cultural traits.

majors—major championships, the most prestigious and important golf tournaments held each year. Golf's four majors are the Masters Tournament in April; the U.S. Open in June; the British Open in July; and the PGA Championship in August.

par—the number of strokes an expert golfer is expected to require to complete a hole; also, the number of strokes required to play an entire course by an expert who makes no mistakes.

prostate cancer—a disease that affects a gland in the male urinary tract, and is often fatal if not treated in time.

putt—a short stroke in which the ball rolls along the ground toward (and ideally into) the hole.

scholarship—money that is awarded to a student to help pay for cost of his or her education. Top athletes often receive scholarships in exchange for their participation on a school's sports teams.

sponsor's exemptions—in professional golf, when a company pays a large fee to underwrite the costs of a tournament, that company is entitled to pick four players to participate in the tournament. Sponsors seek players who can increase the audience, and thus the revenue, of the tournament.

unprecedented—something that has never been done before.

ABOUT THE AUTHOR

Jim Gallagher is the author of more than two dozen books for young adults. He lives in Stockton, New Jersey, with his wife, LaNelle, and their two sons, Dillon and Donald.

Picture Credits

page

 2: Star Max Photos
 6: UPI Photo Archive
 9: Reuters Photo Archive
10: UPI Newspictures
12: Splash News
15: Photographer Showcase
17: Orange County Register/KRT
20: Digital Press Photos
23: UPI Photo Archive
25: Emmanuel Dunand/AFP
26: Digital Press Photos
28: Tom Russo/UPI Photo
30: Icon Sports Photos

33: Splash News
34: UPI Photo Archive
35: Newswire Photo Service
37: Icon Sports Photos
39: Wagner International/FPS
40: WENN Photos
42: New Millennium Images
45: Brian Aho/US Navy/NMI
47: UPI Newspictures
48: Icon Sports Photos
50: International Sports Images
53: Tiger Woods Foundation/KRT
54: Starstock/Photoshot Images

Front cover: Abaca Press/KRT
Back cover: Icon Sports Photos

HAMILTON MIDDLE SCHOOL
139 E. 20TH STREET
HOUSTON, TX 77008